FACILITATOR DISCUSSION GUIDE

SEX, DATING AND RELATING FACILITATOR DISCUSSION GUIDE
Published by Laugh Your Way America! LLC

International Standard Book Number: 978-1-935519-16-4
Mark Gungor, author

ACKNOWLEDGEMENTS

Thanks to Diane Brierley for writing this discussion guide and to Ross Skorzewski for his valuable input as a youth pastor.

TABLE OF CONTENTS

PAGE

SEX, DATING & RELATING

INTRODUCTION

Unless you have been living under a rock in this country, it is very obvious how highly sexualized our society has become. Everywhere the eye can look from TV, magazines, Internet, and movies, to advertising, billboards and even texting on cell phones, we are living in a sex saturated society. The ramifications and consequences to our culture—especially the youth—has yet to play out entirely.

What once was talked about in private and looked at or kept a secret, not to mention hard to get your hands on, is now flowing freely into our homes and into the eyes, hearts and minds of our young people. What used to be considered perverse is now very normal and mainstream to many. So called “sex experts” freely propagate dangerous myth and misinformation. Many people, teens as well as adults, have bought into this culture’s value system and the ideas the media feeds us regarding sex and relationships. It is important to know that the myths and misinformation out there will lead to poor decisions that can have grave—even life-threatening consequences.

Mark Gungor and Laugh Your Way America have put together basic information that every teen needs to know when it comes to the subjects of sex, dating and relating. After years of working with married couples who were struggling in their relationships, he discovered that so often the troubles were rooted in the mistakes that people made during their teen years, which includes premarital sex, serial dating, and becoming physically/emotionally attached to another. Then they break up causing emotional heartache. Then they repeat the cycle to find the validation and get their needs met through another relationship and sexual experimentation have left countless adults with baggage that impacts their marriages and sex lives as adults.

If we equip our students with the right information, we should see better results and spend less time trying to untangle the train wrecks that happen because people continue to make the wrong choices

The DVD set *Sex, Dating and Relating* contains four discs. The first is taken from Mark’s *Laugh Your Way to a Better Marriage*® seminar and includes portions of his “Tale of Two Brains” session. In this section, Mark explains the basic differences in how men and women are wired and how to better understand and work with those differences.

On disc two, Mark explains the keys to dating smart and what to avoid during the process of dating in order to steer clear of trouble.

Disc three contains information on sex from national abstinence speaker Pam Stenzel teaching youth about the consequences of sex outside of marriage as well as Mark explaining more of the emotional impact it can have on people. He also addresses the issue of pornography use and masturbation.

The final disc is a Q & A session with Mark where he answers some of the commonly asked questions regarding sex and dating in his straight-forward manner.

As youth leaders, it is imperative that we get the truth out to the young people in our churches. The church has been silent for far too long on the subject of sex and its consequences; this will continue to be devastating to our culture. It's time to stand up, speak up, educate our youth and engage in the battle against the lies and misinformation rampant in society in order to teach them God's design for living. If we don't step up to this challenge, then we shouldn't be surprised at the results. We will keep creating more broken people due to sexual promiscuity and over-romanticized notions of dating and marriage. We will continue to pay the price with even more dysfunction, broken families and shattered lives.

Sex, Dating and Relating is about helping young people get it right from the beginning, so they can learn to make the best choices in relationships and have successful lives, marriages and families. Without confident, well-equipped teenagers, there won't be strong families in the next generation, and without strong families, the church has no future. The sexual revolution brought much devastation and destruction to our culture. It's time for a new revolution. It's time to teach teens the truth and cut through the lies and garbage that the world is selling them in order to give them a better future.

Discussion Starters for Leaders

The following section contains questions that you can use to facilitate conversation with your group.

We recommend that you watch the DVDs first and preview the information so you can make notes and decide what portions are most important to discuss with your group. It is important talk about these questions with them prior to having them view the *Sex, Dating and Relating* DVDs. This will allow you to gain great insight into their thinking and also expose any misinformation they may have. Then discuss them again after to see how their answers change based on the new information they acquire.

Please note that questions marked with an asterisk (*) are only applicable after viewing. The starter questions provided are just launching pads for your conversation. You and your teens may think of many more.

You may also want to send these questions home so parents can discuss them with their kids. Parents should be the number one filter and source of information in regard to instilling their values in their kids. As a youth leader, you can be the spring board that helps launch the discussion for them.

Q and A time with your group may be a time that sensitive information is revealed regarding personal lives and family situations. It is important to reassure your students that they will not be judged or ridiculed and their answers will be kept confidential. Also, make this rule clearly known to all in the group.

Work as a team to educate your young people. The Appendix in the back of this guide includes useful handouts that you can give to parents to help them in their important role. You may also want to schedule a parent night where you watch the DVD set with just the adults and discuss the information, questions or concerns that they have.

DISC 1 - Relating

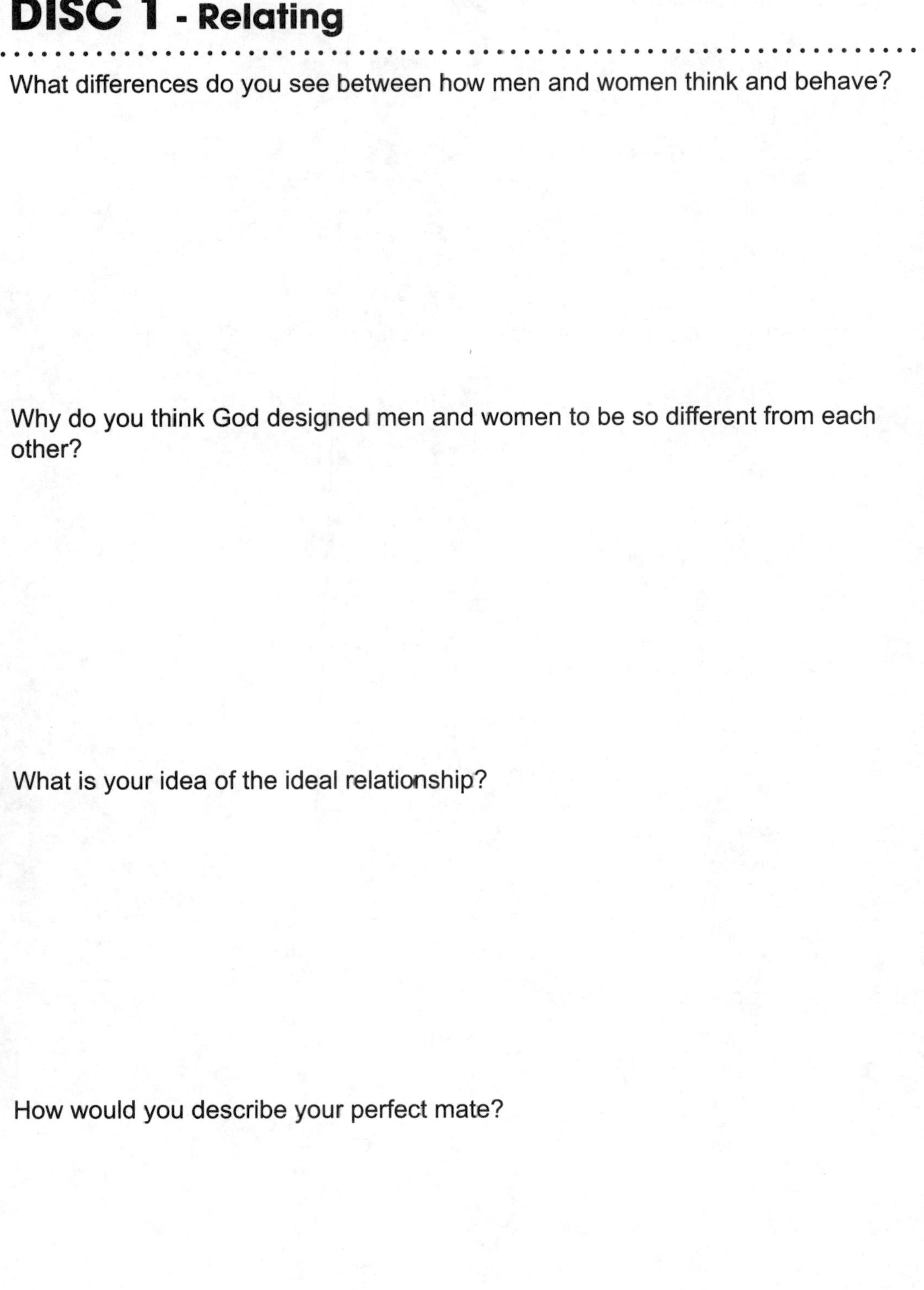

What differences do you see between how men and women think and behave?

Why do you think God designed men and women to be so different from each other?

What is your idea of the ideal relationship?

How would you describe your perfect mate?

I can do everything through him who gives me strength.

Philippians 4:13

SEX, DATING & RELATING

What do you think makes a strong marriage?

Who are your strongest and weakest role models for marriage?

How would you describe "true love"?

What do you consider to be romance?

What does your future look like concerning relationships?

What does conflict look like? How do you handle conflict in relationships? How much conflict do you think is reasonable in a relationship?

What do you think are the hardest things about marriage?

Notes:

.How can a young man keep his way pure? By living according to your word. I seek you with all my heart; do not let me stray from your commands. I have hidden your word in my heart that I might not sin against you.

Psalm 119:9-11

SEX, DATING & RELATING

DISC 2 - Dating

What age do you think is right for you to start dating?

How long should you date before marriage?

What things do you look for when you are deciding to date someone?

How important is the whole "big wedding" to you?

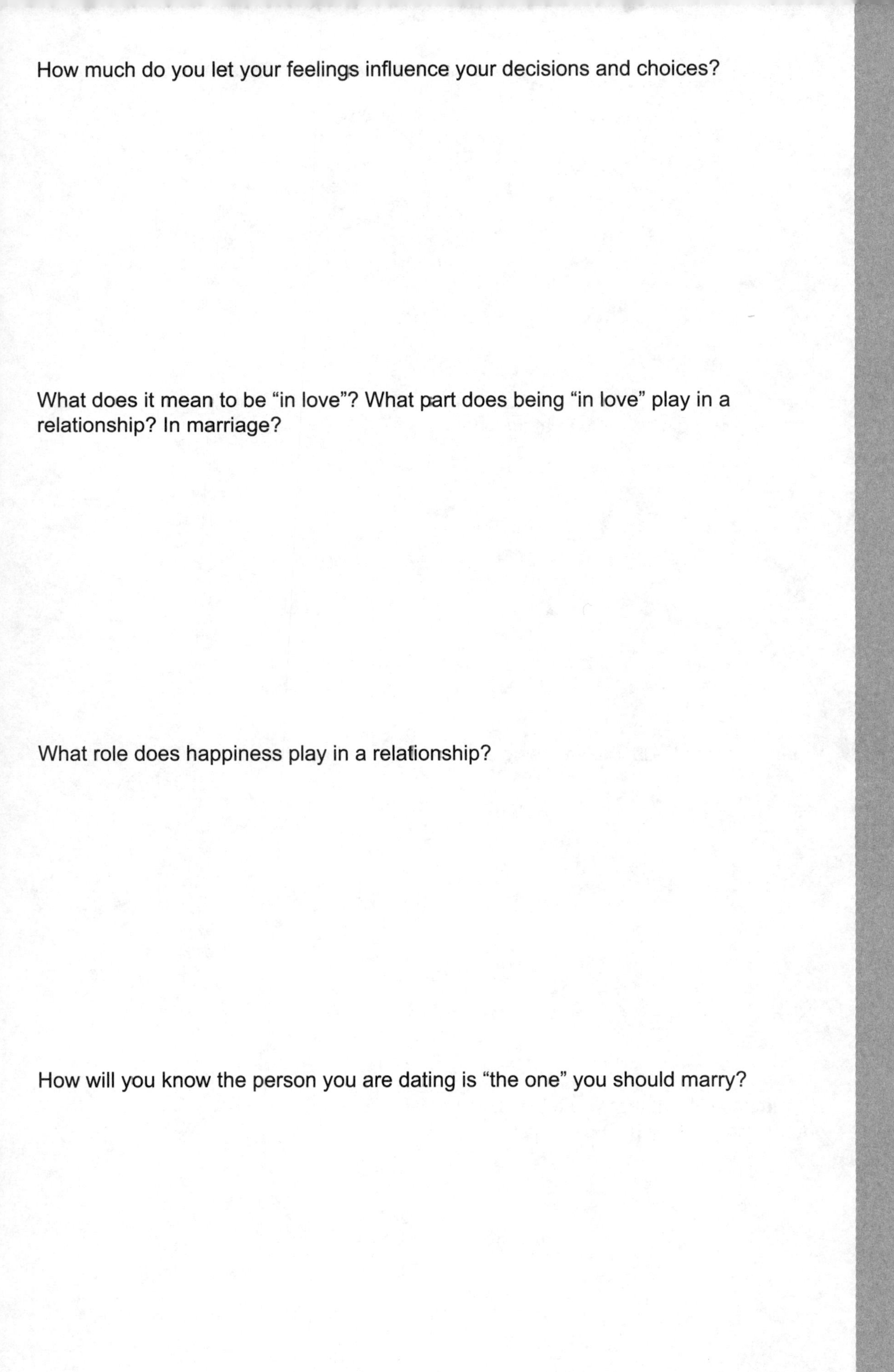

How much do you let your feelings influence your decisions and choices?

What does it mean to be “in love”? What part does being “in love” play in a relationship? In marriage?

What role does happiness play in a relationship?

How will you know the person you are dating is “the one” you should marry?

Parents can provide their sons with an inheritance of houses and wealth, but only the LORD can give an understanding wife.

Proverbs 19:14

Do you believe in "soul mates"? Does God have that one special person just for you?

What is your opinion of "love at first sight"?

When it comes to dating, choosing a mate and marriage, how important is your parents' input to you?

How important is it that you follow God's design for marriage, even if it isn't what your friends, family or society says?

What do you believe is God's perspective and design for dating and marriage?

What are your thoughts on divorce?

What are God's thoughts on divorce?

Notes:

Tune your ears to wisdom, and concentrate on understanding.

Proverbs 2:2

SEX, DATING & RELATING

DISC 3 - Sex

Where do you draw the line when it comes to a physical relationship? How far is too far? What is permissible?

What would you do if your boyfriend/girlfriend was pressuring you to go farther sexually than you wanted to?

How far is too far for God? What does He consider permissible?

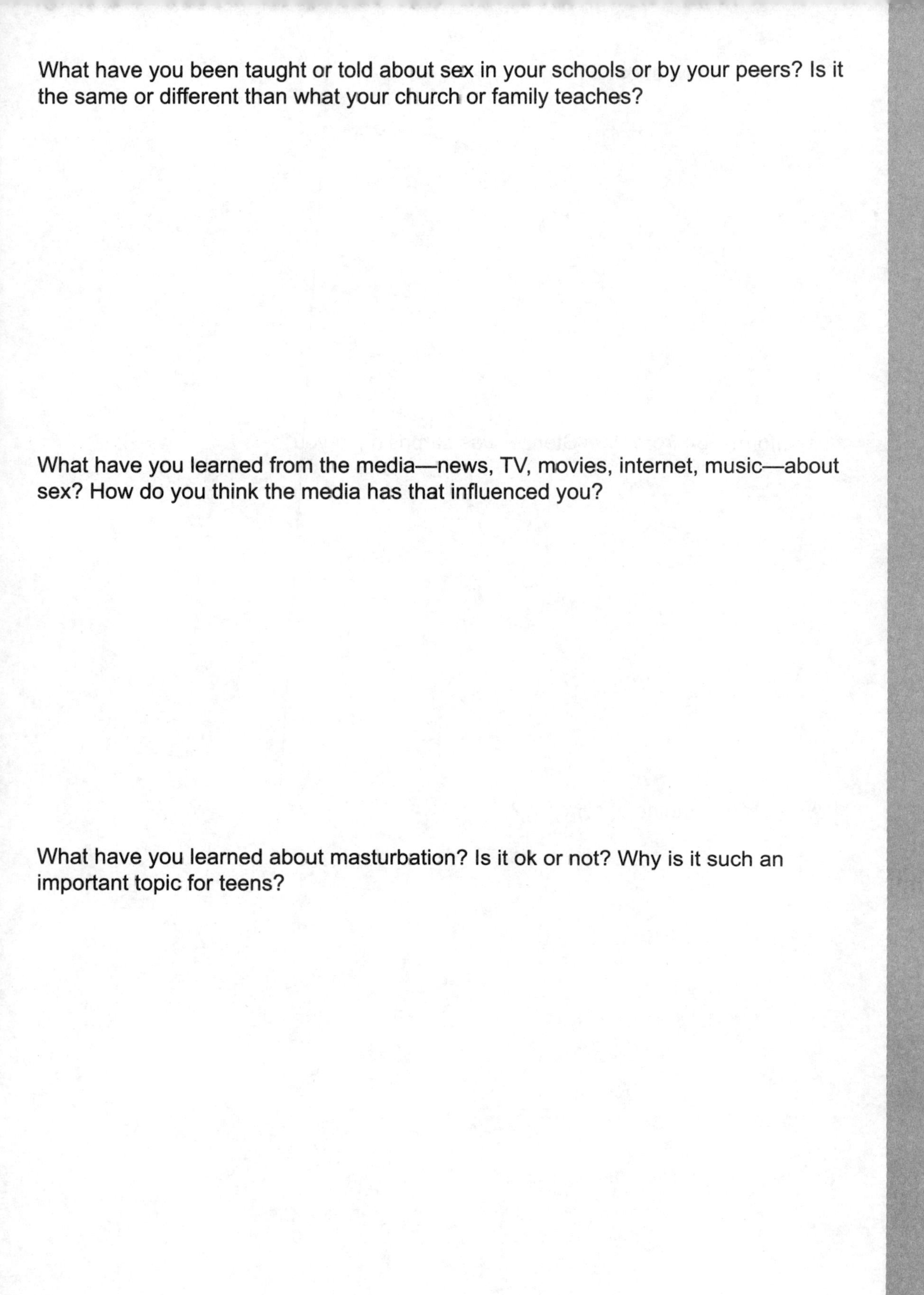

What have you been taught or told about sex in your schools or by your peers? Is it the same or different than what your church or family teaches?

What have you learned from the media—news, TV, movies, internet, music—about sex? How do you think the media has that influenced you?

What have you learned about masturbation? Is it ok or not? Why is it such an important topic for teens?

As iron sharpens iron, so people can improve each other. (NCV) Proverbs 3:13

What do you know about STDs?

What information from Pam Stenzel was surprising to you?*

How would you define abstinence?

What is your definition of sex?

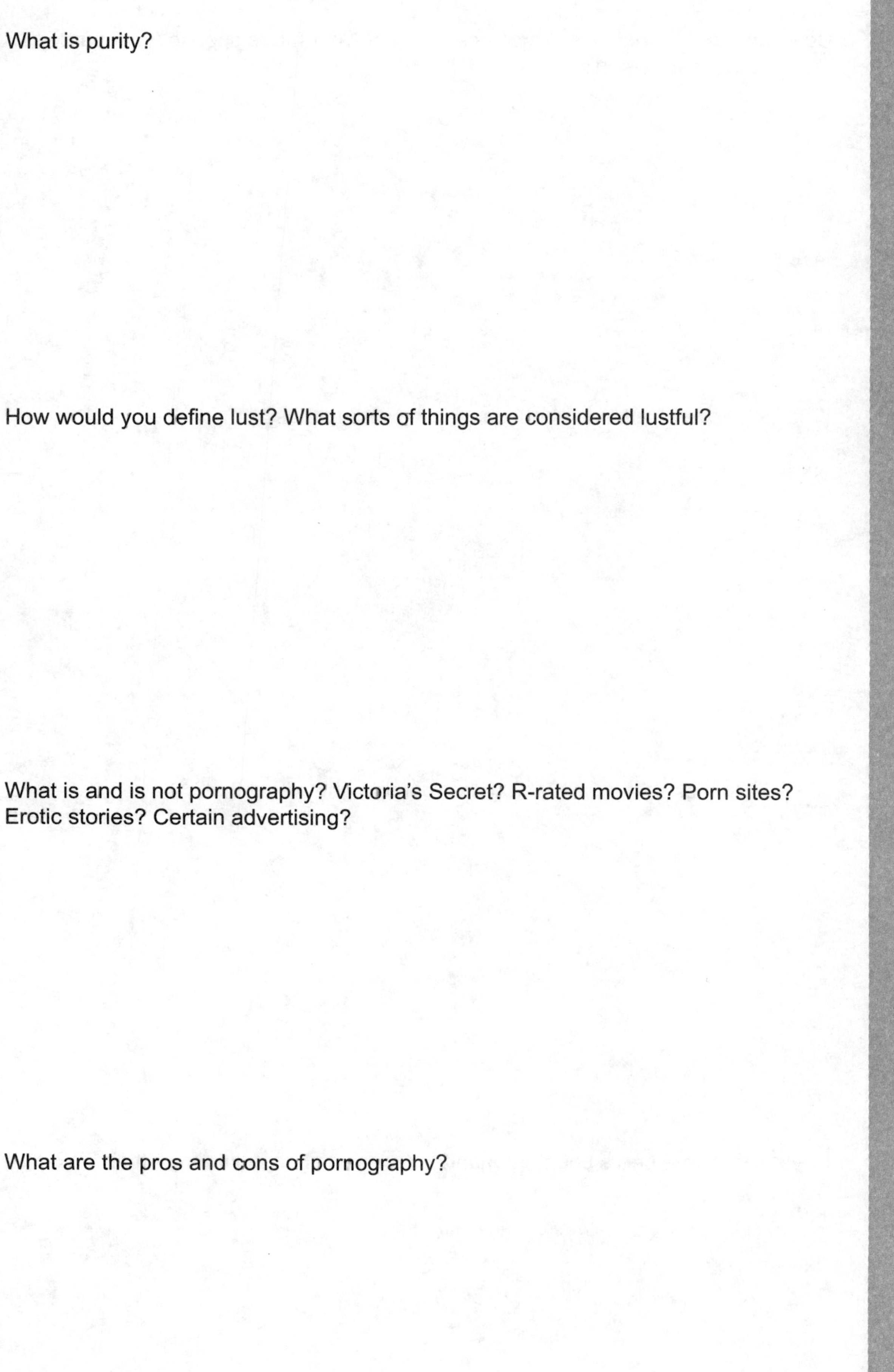

What is purity?

How would you define lust? What sorts of things are considered lustful?

What is and is not pornography? Victoria's Secret? R-rated movies? Porn sites? Erotic stories? Certain advertising?

What are the pros and cons of pornography?

Listen to counsel and receive instruction, that you may eventually become wise.

Proverbs 19:20

How important is purity when it comes to finding your future spouse (your purity as well as the other person's purity)?

What's the overall attitude about sex among your friends?

Are your friends having sex? What are your thoughts about that?

Have any of your peers been pregnant? How has it changed them or their life?

Have any of your peers had an abortion? How has it changed them or their life?

How does teenage pregnancy affect the male in regard to their life and future? How does it affect the female?

Do you think it is unrealistic for a young person to remain a virgin until marriage? Why or why not?

*Above all else,
guard your heart,
for it is the
wellspring of life.*

Proverbs 4:23

How do you know when you are ready to have sex?

What are the benefits of saving yourself and not having sex before marriage?

Notes:

DISC 4 - Q & A

Listed below are the questions from the final disc of the DVD set. As with the questions from the other three discs, it is important to get the students input and answers prior to watching the DVD and before they hear Mark's response to the questions. Follow up each time by comparing and contrasting their answers with Mark's. Did their answers change after they heard his?

How do you deal with the over-sexualized culture that we live in?

How long should you date before marriage?

Why shouldn't a person date someone who is not a Christian?

Put to death, therefore, whatever belongs to your earthly nature: sexual immorality, impurity, lust, evil desires and greed, which is idolatry.

Colossians 3:5

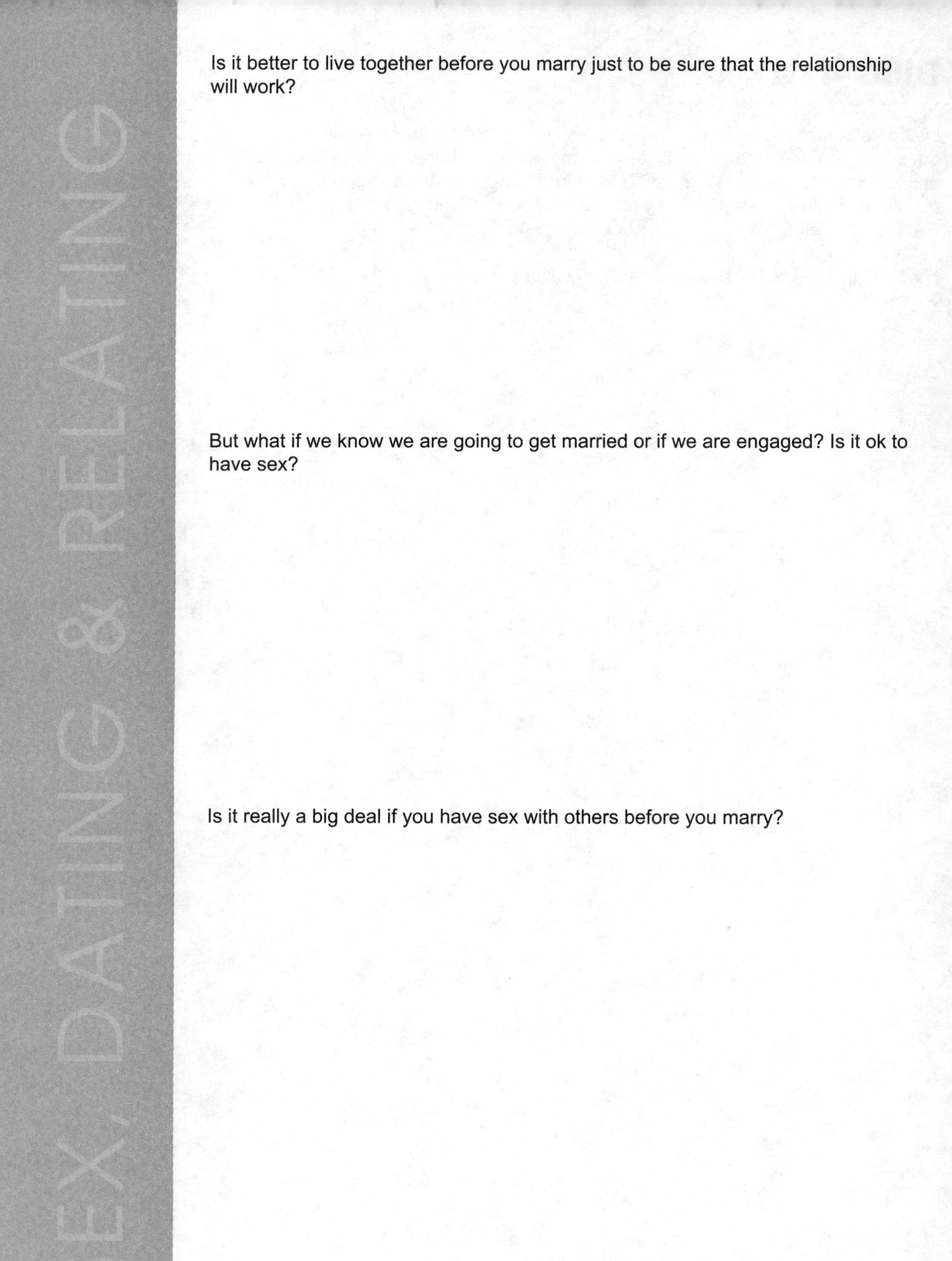

Is it better to live together before you marry just to be sure that the relationship will work?

But what if we know we are going to get married or if we are engaged? Is it ok to have sex?

Is it really a big deal if you have sex with others before you marry?

Isn't it better for teens to be on birth control just in case they don't remain abstinent?

What is the real definition of sex?

Is it expected that girls be the sexually aggressive ones?

But I tell you that anyone who looks at a woman lustfully has already committed adultery with her in his heart.

Matthew 5:28

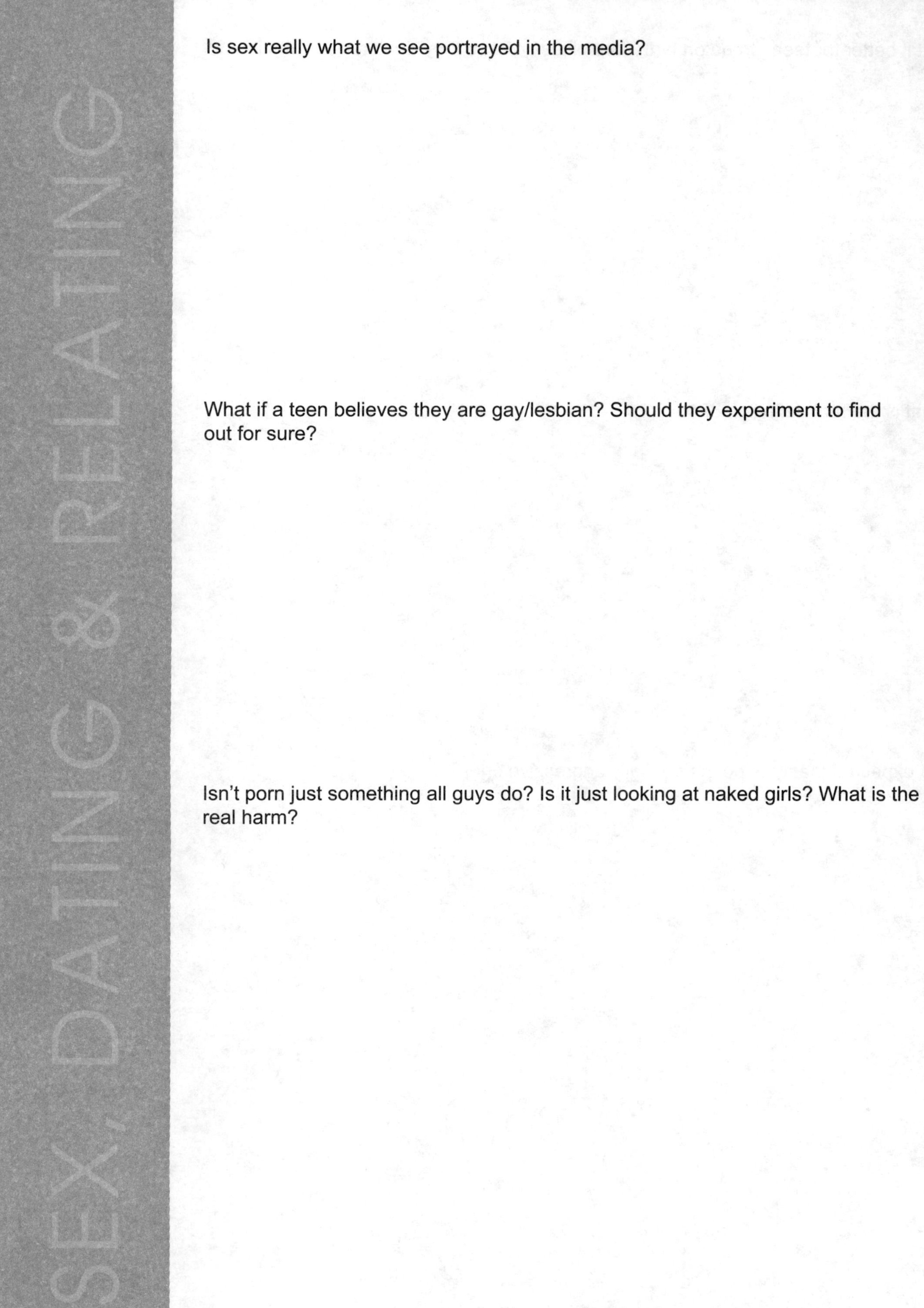

Is sex really what we see portrayed in the media?

What if a teen believes they are gay/lesbian? Should they experiment to find out for sure?

Isn't porn just something all guys do? Is it just looking at naked girls? What is the real harm?

What do you do if you are already into porn and masturbation?

Is there really an escalation that happens when you use pornography?

Notes:

(Love) is not rude, it is not self-seeking, it is not easily angered, it keeps no record of wrongs.

1 Corinthians 13:5

Scripture References for Dating & Relating

Discs One and Two

Psalm 14:4
Where there are no oxen, the manger is empty, but from the strength of an ox comes abundant harvest. (NIV)

Ecclesiastes 4:9-12
9 Two people can accomplish more than twice as much as one; they get a better return for their labor. 10 If one person falls, the other can reach out and help. But people who are alone when they fall are in real trouble. 11 And on a cold night, two under the same blanket can gain warmth from each other. But how can one be warm alone? 12 A person standing alone can be attacked and defeated, but two can stand back-to-back and conquer. Three are even better, for a triple-braided cord is not easily broken. (NLT)

1 Corinthians 7:1
Now for the matters you wrote about, it is good for a man not to marry. (NIV)

1 Corinthians 7:28
But those who marry will face many troubles in this life, and I want to spare you this. (NIV)

Genesis 2:18-24
18 The LORD God said, "It is not good for the man to be alone. I will make a helper suitable for him." 19 Now the LORD God had formed out of the ground all the beasts of the field and all the birds of the air. He brought them to the man to see what he would name them, and whatever the man called each living creature, that was its name. 20 So the man gave names to all the livestock, the birds of the air and all the beasts of the field. But for Adam no suitable helper was found. 21 So the LORD God caused the man to fall into a deep sleep, and while he was sleeping, he took one of the man's ribs and closed up the place with flesh. 22 Then the LORD God made a woman from the rib he had taken out of the man, and he brought her to the man. 23 The man said, "This is now bone of my bones and flesh of my flesh; she shall be called 'woman,' for she was taken out of man." 24 For this reason, a man will leave his father and mother and be united to his wife, and they will become one flesh. (NIV)

Proverbs 19:14
Parents can provide their sons with an inheritance of houses and wealth, but only the LORD can give an understanding wife. (NLT)

Proverbs 27:17
As iron sharpens iron, so people can improve each other. (NCV)

Proverbs 3:13
Blessed is the man who finds wisdom, the man who gains understanding. (NIV)

Proverbs 4:5-7
5 Sell everything and buy wisdom! Forage for understanding! Don't forget one word! Don't deviate an inch! 6 Never walk away from wisdom—she guards your life; love her–she keeps her eye on you. 7 Above all and before all, do this: Get wisdom! Write this at the top of your list: Get understanding! (MSG)

Proverbs 1:5
The wise also will hear and increase in learning, and the person of understanding will acquire skill and attain to sound counsel so that he may be able to steer his course rightly. (AMP)

Proverbs 2:2
Tune your ears to wisdom, and concentrate on understanding. (NIV)

Proverbs 9:6
Forsake foolishness and live, and go in the way of understanding.. (NKJ)

Proverbs 19:20
Listen to counsel and receive instruction that you may eventually become wise. (NAB)

Scripture References for Sex

Disc Three

Job 31:1
I made a covenant with my eyes not to look lustfully at a girl. (NIV)

Proverbs 9:9
Give teaching to a wise man; and he will be even wiser. Teach a man who is right and good, and he will grow in learning. (NLV)

Proverbs 13:16
Wise people think before they act. (NLT)

Hebrews 13:4
Marriage should be honored by all and the marriage bed kept pure; for God will judge the adulterer and all the sexually immoral. (NIV)

Proverbs 4:23
Above all else, guard your heart for it is the wellspring of life. (NIV)

Proverbs 6:27-28
Can a man carry fire in his arms, and his clothes not be burned? 28 Can a man walk on hot coals, and his feet not be burned? (NLV)

Proverbs 9:17-18
Stolen water is sweet. And bread eaten in secret is pleasing. 18 But he does not know that the dead are there, and that the ones who visit her are in the bottom of hell. (NLV)

Matthew 5:28
But I tell you that anyone who looks at a woman lustfully has already committed adultery with her in his heart. (NIV)

1 Thessalonians 4:3-5
It is God's will that you should be sanctified: that you should avoid sexual immorality; 4 that each of you should learn to control his own body in a way that is holy and honorable, 5 not in passionate lust like the heathen, who do not know God; (NIV)

1 Thessalonians 5:11
So encourage each other and build each other up just as you are already doing. (NLT)

1 Corinthians 13:5
(Love) is not rude, it is not self-seeking, it is not easily angered, it keeps no record of wrongs. (NIV)

Colossians 3:5
Put to death, therefore, whatever belongs to your earthly nature: sexual immorality, impurity, lust, evil desires and greed, which is idolatry. (NIV)

Philippians 4:8
Finally, brothers, whatever is true, whatever is noble, whatever is right, whatever is pure, whatever is lovely, whatever is admirable—if anything is excellent or praiseworthy—think about such things.(NIV)

SEX, DATING & RELATING

Scripture to Memorize

The most powerful thing you can do to combat temptation and help you deal with issues of pornography and lust is to memorize scripture. You will have the very Word of God in your heart, like the Bible commands. Memorize these scriptures and be set free. Jesus came not only to forgive you FOR your sins; He came to free you FROM your sin. These scriptures will empower you to live the life Christ died for and intends for you to have. The Word tells us that sin no longer has a hold on us if we are believers in Jesus. Speak these verses when you are dealing with temptation. Fight with the power of the sword and the Word of God just like Jesus did when He faced temptation.

1 Corinthians 10:13
No temptation has seized you except what is common to man. And God is faithful; he will not let you be tempted beyond what you can bear. But when you are tempted, he will also provide a way out so that you can stand up under it. (NIV)

James 1:12-16
Blessed is the man who perseveres under trial because when he has stood the test, he will receive the crown of life that God has promised to those who love him. 13 When tempted, no one should say, “God is tempting me.” For God cannot be tempted by evil, nor does he tempt anyone; 14 but each one is tempted when, by his own evil desire, he is dragged away and enticed. 15 Then, after desire has conceived, it gives birth to sin; and sin, when it is full-grown, gives birth to death. 16 Don’t be deceived, my dear brothers. (NIV)

Psalm 119:9-11
How can a young man keep his way pure?
By living according to your word.
10 I seek you with all my heart;
do not let me stray from your commands.
11 I have hidden your word in my heart
that I might not sin against you. (NIV)

Philippians 4:13
I can do everything through him who gives me strength. (NIV)

James 4:7-8
Submit yourselves, then, to God. Resist the devil, and he will flee from you. 8 Come near to God, and he will come near to you. Wash your hands, you sinners, and purify your hearts, you double-minded. (NIV)

Matthew 1:21
She will give birth to a son, and you are to give him the name Jesus because he will save his people from their sins.” (NIV)

1 John 2:14
I write to you, fathers,
because you have known him who is from the beginning.
I write to you, young men,
because you are strong,
and the word of God lives in you,
and you have overcome the evil one. (NIV)

Hebrews 2:17-18
For this reason, he had to be made like his brothers in every way in order that he might become a merciful and faithful high priest in service to God, and that he might make atonement for the sins of the people. 18 Because he himself suffered when he was tempted, he is able to help those who are being tempted. (NIV)

Hebrews 4:14-16
Therefore, since we have a great high priest who has ascended into heaven, Jesus the Son of God, let us hold firmly to the faith we profess. 15 For we do not have a high priest who is unable to sympathize with our weaknesses, but we have one who has been tempted in every way, just as we are—yet was without sin. 16 Let us then approach the throne of grace with confidence, so that we may receive mercy and find grace to help us in our time of need. (NIV)

Hebrews 4:12-13
For the word of God is living and active. Sharper than any double-edged sword, it penetrates even to dividing soul and spirit, joints and marrow; it judges the thoughts and attitudes of the heart. 13 Nothing in all creation is hidden from God's sight. Everything is uncovered and laid bare before the eyes of him to whom we must give account. (NIV)

Ephesians 6:10-18
Finally be strong in the Lord and in his mighty power. 11 Put on the full armor of God so that you can take your stand against the devil's schemes. 12 For our struggle is not against flesh and blood, but against the rulers, against the authorities, against the powers of this dark world and against the spiritual forces of evil in the heavenly realms. 13 Therefore, put on the full armor of God, so that when the day of evil comes, you may be able to stand your ground, and after you have done everything, to stand. 14 Stand firm then, with the belt of truth buckled around your waist, with the breastplate of righteousness in place, 15 and with your feet fitted with the readiness that comes from the gospel of peace. 16 In addition to all this, take up the shield of faith with which you can extinguish all the flaming arrows of the evil one. 17 Take the helmet of salvation and the sword of the Spirit, which is the word of God. 18 and pray in the Spirit on all occasions with all kinds of prayers and requests. With this in mind, be alert and always keep on praying for all saints.

Appendix: Handouts for Parents

The following pages are for youth leaders to reproduce and give to parents of the teens in your group. Encourage parents to follow up with their kids at home and discuss the videos they watched, as well as the discussion your group had. Also, encourage your students to engage in the conversation with their mom/dad/guardian. It is important that they have open lines of communication in all areas with their parents, especially when it comes to dating and sex.

Talking About Sex & Dating With Your Teens

Parents need to be the number one source of their kids' sex education. Moms and dads should never leave that job up to schools, teachers, youth pastors or worse, their friends and the media that surround our young people with over-sexualized messages and bad information.

Many parents are nervous and uncomfortable talking about sex with their kids. Often they worry that if they talk about it, kids will "get ideas" and be more likely to engage in sexual activity, but that is not the case. If you aren't talking to your kids and teaching them, it is guaranteed that others are. It is vitally important that you give them the facts and the truth that they will not hear from the culture that we live in. It is the job of parents to counter the lies and the dangerous information that saturates young people in their world.

Talking to your teens about sex, dating, and relating can be just as hard for you, the parent, as it can be for your kids. We want to help make it easier for you.

Often parents plan to talk about sex with their children but somehow just never manage to bring up the subject. The reality is, your child will learn about sex, either from you, or from someone else. Keep in mind that it's not about having "The Talk" like so many parents think. Sex and dating are topics that you need to constantly revisit with your kids as they grow and face the challenges and changes of puberty, adolescence and into early adulthood.

The following are some pointers to help make the discussion easier.

1. Clearly communicate your values and expectations about sex. Explain your values in a caring, yet firm way and look for opportunities to repeat the message. Setting high standards based on your personal values and those of your faith community will make an impression that facts and figures alone cannot make. Tell your children what you believe they are capable of; their actions will often rise to meet your expectations.

2. Make sure your actions match your words. It is important to model positive relationships and healthy habits not just talk about them. Your child will respect your opinions and advice the most if you are a good role model.

3. Encourage open communication about sex at a young age. Talking about sex, puberty and relationships will be easier if you begin early and continue communicating as your child matures. Start using the correct names for body parts and answering basic questions such as "Where do babies come from?" as simply and honestly as possible at a young age. Keep communication open by initiating conversations about sex and relationships as the topics arise in the media or with friends and family.

4. Be accessible, approachable and willing to listen. Showing respect for your child by listening is a good way to open up communication. If you make a habit of listening to your child and inquiring about the "little things" like school, friends and activities, your child will be more likely to come to you with questions and concerns about sex and other tough issues. Honest answers build a foundation for your child to see you as the resource for sexual information in the future.

5. Make information available. Have adolescent-friendly books, videos and pamphlets around the house for your children to review when they choose. Remember, the less you push, the more likely they are to seek out answers to their questions.

6. Be involved in your child's school. Do you know what your children are learning about sex in school? Find out when presentations on sex and related topics will be given at your child's school and ask for information about the presentation or to review the material that will be used. If you don't feel this information is appropriate, find a healthy, positive alternative curriculum and encourage the instructor and administration to use it. Remember, you are the authority in your child's life, especially concerning values, including sexuality.

7. Remember that sex is good and hormones are real. Curiosity about sex will not go away if it is never discussed. In fact, avoiding the subject can make sex seem even more mysterious and exciting. Be sure to balance discussions by talking about the positive aspects of sex within marriage as well as the responsibilities that come with it.

8. Point out the positive. There is a direct link between low self-esteem and high-risk behaviors such as drug use, early sexual involvement, and other self-destructive behaviors. Compliment your children when they are doing what is right and help them set positive goals for the future. Help your children build self-esteem based on character, unique talents and positive accomplishments. Make sure to show your appreciation and pride for all they do right before offering constructive criticism about what to avoid. When they make mistakes, talk about how to earn back your trust. Never leave them feeling hopeless.

9. Give your child good reasons for making positive, healthy choices. Adolescents tend to make decisions based on feelings instead of logic and experience. Often, they believe they know everything and can be hurt by nothing. Their attitude is, "I need it now!" If we want adolescents to make good decisions about their futures, we must give them practical reasons they can relate to for making choices that will lead to health and happiness. For example, it's hard to run track if you're six months pregnant. If your children have made poor decisions, encourage them to start over and move in a more positive direction.

10. Know the facts and share them in a positive way. Attempting to influence your child's behavior by focusing on guilt and fear may have the opposite effect — rebellion. Instead, know the facts about teen pregnancy, sexually transmitted diseases (STDs), and puberty, and share them with your child in a non-threatening way. Parents who set high standards are offering their child the best protection against high-risk behaviors.

Excerpted from "Sex Q&A: Kids' Questions — Parents' Answers," published by National Physicians Center for Family Resources. Copyright © 2007 National Physicians Center for Family Resources.

Finding the Teachable Moments

Teaching moments often occur when least expected, so be prepared. Be open to any discussion, and do not go off the deep end no matter what your child asks. Give a calm, honest answer. Avoid using a preachy or commanding tone.
Recognize an opportunity when it presents itself:

1. If you see something while watching a movie together, and you feel it merits discussion, seize the opportunity.

2. When something happens in the life of one of your kids' friends, use it as a conversation starter.

3. If your son or daughter tells you about a teen pregnancy in her school, capitalize on the situation and use it for discussion and teaching.

4. At a time your kids seems receptive to conversation, ask them if they have any questions about dating or sex. If you get the eye roll, just continue on and make your point.

5. An excellent time to bring up the subject of dating and expectations is immediately after the school has studied sex education in class.

6. Any time a sibling is having trouble on the dating scene, or parents are having difficulties with an older child over the subject of dating, the younger children are watching. Use tumultuous times in your family to feed dating expectation information to the younger siblings, but do so without trespassing on the older child's privacy.

7. Make your job easier by talking with your children at a young age about dating rules, etiquette, etc. You don't have to wait until they hit the teenage years to begin discussing the subject.

8. For some children, darkness seems to bring anonymity and loosens one's tongue. When your son or daughter is ready to turn the light out, sit on the edge of the bed for a "how was your day" talk. You'll be surprised what subjects these conversations can bring about.

Adapted from: "A parent's guide to discussing dating: teenage daughters". By Karen Ray ©2002 Pagewise.

Tips for Talking to Your Teens

TIMING IS EVERYTHING

Know that teens will catch us off guard when they decide to ask questions about sex or other "tough" topics. Resist the urge to flee. Try saying, "I'm glad you came to me with that question." This gives us time to think of a response and will let teens know they can come to parents for advice. It's important to answer the question right away, rather than put off a teen by saying something like – "you're too young to know that!" Chances are, the subject has already come up at school and they're already getting "advice" from their friends. When teens ask questions, look at it as an opportunity to help them learn by sharing our thoughts.

PRACTICE MAKES PERFECT

As parents, anticipation is our best friend. Anticipate what teens' questions may be about sex and dating, then think about your responses ahead of time. What should I say? It's different for each family, but you should become familiar with typical questions and behaviors that occur during the teen years. Do a little digging around popular teen Web sites to find out what's hot in a teen's world.

IS IT HOT IN HERE?

If you're feeling embarrassed or uncomfortable about a question your teen asks, say so. Acknowledging your own discomfort allows your kids to acknowledge theirs – and may make everyone feel a little less awkward all around. It's also okay for parents to set limits. For example, you do not have to give specific answers about your own teen behaviors.

STICK TO THE BASICS

Teens know hundreds of names for various body parts that would make us blush. We shouldn't try to be cool by using these "hip" terms when talking to teens about tough topics. It won't work. Stick with specific and correct terminology that everyone understands.

INITIATE THE CONVERSATION

When our kids were young, we didn't wait until they asked if they should look both ways before crossing a busy street. We taught them. Now, it's our job to teach teens how to grow into adulthood by educating them. Decide what is important for your teens to know, and then teach them early and often. Use every day, naturally occurring events to initiate conversations with teens about tough topics. For example, books, news articles and TV shows can be good discussion starters.

WATCH FOR HIDDEN MEANING

Be aware of the "question behind the question." Keep your radar up and trust your instincts - if you sense your teen is dealing with a larger issue, you're probably right.

BE CLEAR ABOUT YOUR VALUES

This doesn't mean "be judgmental." Teens (although they will protest) want to and should know their family's values around sexual issues, dating, etc.

RESEARCH THE SOURCES
Know what is taught about teen issues in your schools, churches, temples and youth groups – and use this information as a way to talk with teens about your family's values. You should be your kid's primary teacher in these areas; don't leave it to the school or the church.

ACT NOW
Better "too much, too soon" than "too little, too late." Talking to teens about tough issues in an open, honest and loving manner shouldn't cause fear, nor does it lead to experimentation among teens. Teens are hearing about sex and dating everywhere else. They deserve to hear it from us.

Adapted from: "Kids Need to Know", Family Sexual Education, OR and "Now What Do I Do?" By Robert Selverston, Ph.D.

Bible Translations Used

Pastor Mark and Debbie Gungor

Mark Gungor is the CEO of Laugh Your Way America and Senior Pastor of Celebration Church. Married to Debbie for more than 35 years, he is also the creator of the highly regarded Laugh Your Way to a Better Marriage® seminar. Mark believes that the key to a successful marriage is not about finding the right person; it's about doing the right things. If you do the right things you will succeed, if you don't, you'll fail. It's just that simple. Our goal is to help couples get along, get it right, have fun and achieve a successful marriage. Laugh Your Way America exists to eliminate divorce in America, one family at a time.

Laugh Your Way America!, LLC
3475 Humboldt Road
Green Bay, WI 54311
866-525-2844
www.laughyourway.com

Teen Resources

Below you will find a selection of resources that Mark references in the DVD set, as well as some we've found across the web that you may find useful as a teen or in talking with your teen. Please note, all links take you to sites beyond our control, resources were relevant and appropriate at the time we added them, but may have changed since. Please check our web page at http://www.sexdatingandrelating.com for the most recent links and resources we have available.

Hooked: New Science on How Casual Sex is Affecting Our Children A book by M.D. Joe S. McIlhaney Jr. and M.D. Freda McKissic Bush that shows how the bonds of sexual relationships can have serious consequences.

Cohabitation Facts Research that shows that cohabitation is detrimental to successful relationships for adults and especially harmful for children. http://www.citizenlink.org/FOSI/marriage/cohabitation/A000007333.cfm

"Did I Get Married Too Young?" A writer for the Wall Street Journal discusses the "problems" of marrying young and how it's affected his life. http://online.wsj.com/article/SB10001424052748704107204575039150739864666.html

"Don't Wait for Marriage" Article from John Van Epp that shows young adults should start searching for a spouse sooner rather than later. http://www.uscatholic.org/dontwait

The Case Against Adolescence: Rediscovering the Adult in Every Teen and
Teen 2.0: Saving Our Children and Families from the Torment of Adolescence
Two books by Robert Epstein that show the detrimental effects extended adolescence has on teens and our culture.

Benefits of Abstinence Research from the Kaiser Family Foundation that shows individuals who remain abstinent through their teens years make more money and have a lower divorce rate. http://www.kaisernetwork.org/daily_reports/rep_index.cfm?hint=2&DR_ID=29873

"Life in thin slices: An ancient smile may predict a modern divorce" Article from The Economist that shows the connection between a good smile and a good marriage. http://www.depauw.edu/learn/lab/media/documents/media/22_The_Economist_2009_story.pdf

"Masturbation May Increase Risk of Prostate Cancer" Study that shows the possible connection between the two. http://www.livescience.com/health/090126-masturbation-prostate.html

Muslim Demographics The YouTube video that portrays the demographics of the Christian population compared to Muslims. http://www.youtube.com/watch?v=6-3X5hIFXYU

"Oxytocin, the Real Love Potion #9" Research is showing this hormone is one secret to a happy marriage, dubbed the "cuddle hormone," it has crucial influence on a couple's bonding. http://www.abstinence.net/library/index.php?entryid=2490

"Say Yes. What Are You Waiting For?" Article from the Washington Post that gives the reasons for early marriage. http://www.washingtonpost.com/wp-dyn/content/article/2009/04/24/AR2009042402122.html

"Sex with a Partner is 400% Better" Research shows that there is a biological difference between solo-sex and that with a spouse. http://www.newscientist.com/article/mg18925405.900-sex-with-a-partner-is-400-better.html

Talk It Out Before You Say, "I Do" Do you really know your potential spouse as well as you think? Are there areas you need to know about (or they need to know about you) that you haven't discussed? A great list of questions to start pre-marriage conversation. http://www.cbn.com/family/marriage/ferwerda-before-I-do.aspx

"The Case for Early Marriage" Article from Christianity Today that says amid our purity pledges and attempts to make chastity hip, we forgot to teach young Christians how to tie the knot. http://www.cbn.com/family/marriage/ferwerda-before-I-do.aspx

"The Effectiveness of Abstinence Education Programs in Reducing Sexual Activity Among Youth" This report from The Heritage Foundation examines abstinence education. http://www.heritage.org/Research/Reports/2002/04/The-Effectiveness-of-Abstinence-Education-Programs

"The Harmful Effects of Early Sexual Activity and Multiple Sexual Partners among Women" This report from The Heritage Foundation that examines the linkages between early initiation of sexual activity, number of non- marital sex partners, and human well-being. http://www.heritage.org/Research/Reports/2003/06/Harmful-Effects-of-Early-Sexual-Activity-and-Multiple-Sexual-Partners-Among-Women-Charts

"Virgins Make the Best Valentines" Article on why virgins have lasting marriages. http://article.nationalreview.com/print/?q=MGNiODQ4YmEzMjc1ODc1YTYwNmIxM2Q5ZWZkZmE3YTM=

"Was the Cowardly Lion Just Masturbating Too Much?" Psychology Today article that shows there may be a correlation between porn and social anxiety. http://www.psychologytoday.com/blog/cupids-poisoned-arrow/201001/was-the-cowardly-lion-just-masturbating-too-much

"The Porn Myth" New York Magazine article by Naomi Wolf that examines how porn turns men off from the real thing. http://nymag.com/nymetro/news/trends/n_9437/

The Flag Page® Solution

Now that you've discovered your child's heart, it's time you discover the great things God has in store for you by creating your own Flag Page®. The Flag Page® is an incredible online program designed to help you discover who you are, what you love the most about life and most importantly...who God created you to be.

The entire assessment takes 10 minutes and is great for teens, parents, grandparents, co-workers…the list goes on and on. To get started, log onto www.flagpage.com. It's inexpensive, easy and life-changing.

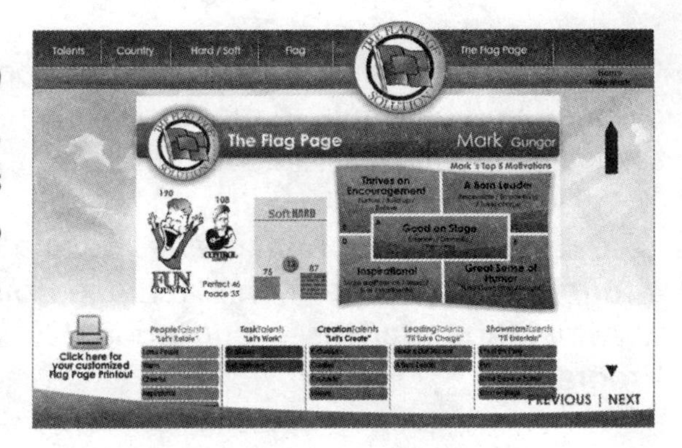

Discovering Your Heart with the Flag Page®

In his book Discovering Your Heart with the Flag Page®, national marriage speaker Mark Gungor explains how to interpret and understand the colorful printout that is the Flag Page®. He shows the reader how to understand why they act and react the way they do, and what important needs they have in their life that are the keys to their success and happiness.

Order your copy at www.laughyourway.com

www.flagpage.com

Laugh Your Way to a Better Marriage

For the first time ever, the entire life-changing Laugh Your Way to a Better Marriage Event is available on DVD!

Filmed in Phoenix, Arizona, this 4-Disc DVD set includes every minute of Mark Gungor's weekend seminar, as well as an extra DVD featuring Mark answering the questions he couldn't cover during the original taping. With over 6 hours of material, the DVD set captures all the fun and facts of Mark's look at life, love, and marriage. Mark will walk you through from beginning to end as you laugh, learn and realize you can make immediate positive change in your own marriage. Perfect for couples, singles and youth, this set makes a great gift. From "The Tale of Two Brains" to the funny, hard-hitting, and must-hear information in "The Number One Key to Incredible Sex", Mark will have you laughing your way to a better marriage in no time!

Sex, Dating & Relating - Teen Edition

As Mark travels the country speaking on the subject of marriage, many have said, "I wish I'd known this when I was younger. Do you have this information for my kids or grandkids?"

Here is the highly anticipated and much sought after information on dating and sex that we all wish we had known growing up. In the society and culture we live in today, it is more important than ever that parents and teens are armed with the real facts and the truth. It's time to cut through all the nonsense that is taught in the media, the education system and even the Church.

Together, Mark and Pam Stenzel bring parents and teens the hard-hitting, no-nonsense wisdom not often heard in the secular or faith culture today. Messages that will help teens and their families make wise decisions enabling the next generation to build strong and successful marriages and families…without all the physical and emotional baggage.

These and many more resources are all available at www.laughyourway.com

Listen to the Mark Gungor Show LIVE Monday - Friday from 10:00am - 11:00am Central Time. Join Mark as he discusses any and all issues concerning live, love and marriage.

www.markgungorshow.com

NOTES

NOTES

NOTES

NOTES